EARTH DETECTIVES

EXPLORING
FOSSILS

PALEONTOLOGISTS AT WORK!

ELSIE OLSON

Consulting Editor, Diane Craig, M.A./Reading Specialist

Super Sandcastle

An Imprint of Abdo Publishing
abdopublishing.com

abdopublishing.com

Printed in the United States of America, North Mankato, Minnesota

102017
012018

THIS BOOK CONTAINS
RECYCLED MATERIALS

Design: Kelly Doudna, Mighty Media, Inc.
Production: Mighty Media, Inc.
Editor: Jessie Alkire
Cover Photographs: iStockphoto; Shutterstock; Wikimedia Commons
Interior Photographs: iStockphoto; Roland Tanglao/Wikimedia Commons; Ryan Somma/Wikimedia Commons; Shutterstock; Wikimedia Commons

Publisher's Cataloging-in-Publication Data

Names: Olson, Elsie, author.
Title: Exploring fossils: paleontologists at work! / by Elsie Olson.
Other titles: Paleontologists at work!
Description: Minneapolis, Minnesota : Abdo Publishing, 2018. | Series: Earth detectives |
Identifiers: LCCN 2017946512 | ISBN 9781532112300 (lib.bdg.) | ISBN 9781614799726 (ebook)
Subjects: LCSH: Paleontology--Juvenile literature. | Fossils--Juvenile literature. |
    Occupations--Juvenile literature. | Earth sciences--Juvenile literature.
Classification: DDC 560--dc23
LC record available at https://lccn.loc.gov/2017946512

Super SandCastle™ books are created by a team of professional educators, reading specialists, and content developers around five essential components—phonemic awareness, phonics, vocabulary, text comprehension, and fluency—to assist young readers as they develop reading skills and strategies and increase their general knowledge. All books are written, reviewed, and leveled for guided reading, early reading intervention, and Accelerated Reader™ programs for use in shared, guided, and independent reading and writing activities to support a balanced approach to literacy instruction.

CONTENTS

WHAT IS A FOSSIL?

A fossil is the remains or traces of living things. The remains are preserved in rock. Fossils take at least 10,000 years to form. Some take millions!

There are two kinds of fossils. Body fossils are petrified remains of plants or animals. The remains can also be frozen or dried. Dinosaur bones are body fossils. Trace fossils are ancient signs of plants or animals. Footprints are trace fossils.

Body fossils

WHO STUDIES FOSSILS?

Paleontologists are scientists who study fossils. They learn what Earth was like long ago.

Paleontologists study how plants and animals change. This helps them learn how Earth might change in the future. Fossils provide clues.

Many fossils are the remains of fish.

Paleontologists usually specialize in and study certain animals or plants. Some focus on dinosaurs!

MARY ANNING

Mary Anning was one of the first paleontologists. She lived on the Dorset Coast. This is in southwestern England. The area is known for having fossils.

Mary's family was poor. Her father died when she was 11. After, Mary and her family gathered fossils. They sold fossils to collectors.

The Dorset Coast is the most popular place in the United Kingdom to find fossils. The area is often called the Jurassic Coast! People still find fossils there today.

FABULOUS FINDS

In 1811, Anning and her brother found something. It was an **ichthyosaur** skeleton! Later, Anning found the first **plesiosaur**. Anning's work was **dangerous**. She climbed up and down cliffs. She searched beaches.

Plesiosaur skull

Many scientists studied Anning's finds. But female scientists were rare. So Anning was often not given credit.

MARY ANNING

BORN: May 21, 1799, Lyme Regis, England

MARRIED: Never married

CHILDREN: None

DIED: March 9, 1847, Lyme Regis, England

FINDING FOSSILS

Paleontologists travel the world looking for fossils. Most fossils are found in **sedimentary** rock.

Erosion is often caused by water.

Some fossils are underground. Paleontologists dig to find them. Other fossils are on the surface. **Erosion** wore away the rock above them.

Rock must be the right age to contain fossils. Most fossils are found in rock that is thousands or millions of years old.

The Rocky Mountains have rock that is millions of years old.
That is the right age for some dinosaur bone fossils!

DIGGING UP

Once a fossil is found, the hard work begins. It is removed from the ground. Fossils are **fragile**. It can take months to remove fossils!

Fossils can be leaves, shells, or bugs. Others are bones or teeth. Paleontologists try to find out what type of plant or animal fossils came from.

Leaf fossils

Diggers work slowly and carefully. They try to keep fossils from breaking. But if fossils break, they can be repaired with glue.

STUDYING FOSSILS

Most fossils are moved to labs in universities and museums. There, paleontologists clean the fossils. They make casts of bones. Scientists study the casts. This way, they won't harm the original.

Scientists ask questions as they study. They ask how old the fossil may be. They figure out where it falls in the fossil record. This is the collection of all Earth's fossils.

A PALEONTOLOGIST'S TOOL KIT

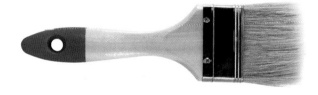

HAMMER AND CHISEL
These are used to chip fossils out of rock.

BRUSH
Scientists brush dirt and rock from fossils.

Paleontologists use tools to dig up and study fossils.

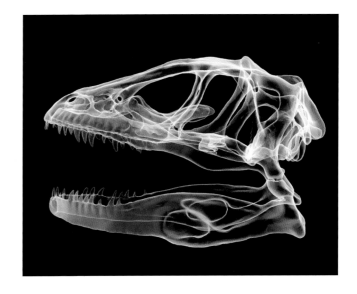

GPS
GPS devices keep paleontologists from getting lost. They also record where fossils are found.

X-RAY MACHINES
X-ray machines show the inside of fossils.

FUTURE FINDS

New fossils are found all the time! In 2015, scientists found part of a dinosaur tail. It was in **amber**. The tail had feathers!

New tools are also being made. They make it easier to find and share fossils. Fossils can be **3-D** printed. Scientists use lasers to scan fossils. A computer then creates **virtual** fossils. Scientists can share the scans **online**.

FOSSILS AND FOAM

AM CUT-OUT

Spinosaurus is known from
ial specimens, adult and
sate an accurate rendering,
were CT-scanned. Digital
fossils were adjusted to
ed to create a composite
s finished digital model
g bit of a cutting
rved an adult skull
ks of foam.

fle guides the bit to
ve a skull from foam.

JAW IN FOAM
(cast)

Touch this foam jaw to feel the
extra ridges left by the first pass
of the machine bit. Later passes
fine tune the surface of the jaw.

3-D PRINT

All bones of the
Spinosaurus and
were CT-scanne
created for eve
printed in plast
was used to
adult skelet

MakerBot Replicator Z18

The digi
1-6th (1

BECOME A PALEONTOLOGIST!

Do you dream of becoming a paleontologist? Here are some things you can do now!

TAKE SCIENCE AND MATH CLASSES. Studying fossils involves math and science. Getting good grades in those classes now will help you in the future.

VISIT A DIG! Some dig sites let students visit. You can watch diggers at work. You might even get a chance to dig!

ASK QUESTIONS! Good scientists ask a lot of questions. They look for new ways to find answers. You can get started now!

TEST YOUR KNOWLEDGE

1. What kind of fossils are footprints?

2. What are scientists who study fossils called?

3. Mary Anning discovered the first **plesiosaur** skeleton. TRUE OR FALSE?

THINK ABOUT IT!

Have you ever seen a fossil at a museum? What did it look like?

ANSWERS: 1. Trace fossils 2. Paleontologists 3. True

GLOSSARY

amber – a sticky orange liquid from trees.

dangerous – able or likely to cause harm or injury.

erosion – the wearing away of rock, especially by wind or water.

fragile – easily broken.

global positioning system (GPS) – a space-based navigation system used to pinpoint locations on Earth.

ichthyosaur – an extinct large sea reptile similar to a fish.

online – connected to the Internet.

plesiosaur – an extinct large sea reptile with a long neck and tail.

sedimentary – rock made from layers of sediments pressed together.

3-D – having three dimensions, such as length, width, and height.

virtual – existing only on computers or the Internet.

X-ray – an invisible and powerful light wave that can pass through solid objects.